All-Star Players

MEET CALVIN JOHNSON

Football's Megatron

Ethan Edwards

PowerKiDS press
New York

Published in 2014 by The Rosen Publishing Group, Inc.
29 East 21st Street, New York, NY 10010

First Edition

Editor: Jennifer Way and Joshua Shadowens
Book Design: Greg Tucker
Book Layout: Andrew Povolny
Photo Research: Katie Stryker

Photo Credits: Cover, pp. 1, 7, 17, 23, 29 Mark Cunningham/Getty Images Sports/Getty Images; p. 4 Gregory Shamus/Getty Images Sports/Getty Images; p. 8 Norm Hall/Stringer/Getty Images Sports/Getty Images; pp. 9, 24 Leon Halip/Stringer/Getty Images Sports/Getty Images; pp. 10, 14–16 Rob Tringali/Sportschrome/ Contributor/Getty Images; p. 12 Scott Halleran/Getty Images Sports/Getty Images; p. 13 Scott Cunningham/ Getty Images Sports/Getty Images; p. 15 Sporting News Archive/Sporting News/Getty Images; pp. 18–19, 20 Chris Graythen/Getty Images Sports/Getty Images; p. 21 Tom Dahlin/Getty Images Sports/Getty Images; p. 25 Joe Robbins/Getty Images Sports/Getty Images; p. 26 David Livingston/Getty Images Entertainment/ Getty Images.

Library of Congress Cataloging-in-Publication Data

Edwards, Ethan.
Meet Calvin Johnson : football's megatron / by Ethan Edwards.
     pages cm. — (All-star players)
Includes index.
ISBN 978-1-4777-2917-5 (library) — ISBN 978-1-4777-3006-5 (pbk.) —
ISBN 978-1-4777-3077-5 (6-pack)
1. Johnson, Calvin, 1985-—Juvenile literature. 2. Football players—United States—Biography—Juvenile literature. I. Title.
GV939.J6123E38 2014
796.332092—dc23
[B]
                              2013027473

Manufactured in the United States of America

CPSIA Compliance Information: Batch #W14PK2: For Further Information contact Rosen Publishing, New York, New York at 1-800-237-9932

Contents

Here is Calvin Johnson during a 2012 game against the Atlanta Falcons. As a wide receiver, Johnson's job is to catch the ball down the field and try to score.

Megatron

Football players are afraid to play against Calvin Johnson of the Detroit Lions. That is because he is one of the biggest **wide receivers** in the National Football League, or NFL. He is also one of the NFL's best wide receivers. In fact, many experts and players believe he could go down in history as the best ever.

Johnson earned the nickname Megatron for being bigger, faster, and fiercer than almost anyone else on the field. Megatron is the most-feared robot in the Transformers movies, TV show, and line of toys.

All-Star Facts

Johnson appeared on the cover of the *Madden NFL 13* video game. Only the best players in the NFL are featured on the covers of the Madden NFL games.

Bigger and Better

Calvin Johnson was born in the town of Newnan, Georgia, on September 29, 1985. The closest big city is Atlanta, and Calvin was a big fan of all the Atlanta sports teams as a kid. He also loved to play sports and proved himself an excellent **athlete** at a young age. Calvin liked football best, but his mother did not let him play because the sport can be dangerous.

Different college recruiters and sports writers agreed that Johnson was one of the top 100 high-school players out of the thousands of players in the country.

As a high-school player, Calvin Johnson's stats got better every year that he played. Here he is catching a pass for the Lions in 2012.

Calvin grew fast. He became a very big kid. He was 6 feet (1.8 m) tall by the time he was just 12 years old. His mother decided that Calvin deserved a chance to play football. It is a good thing he got that chance. Calvin kept growing. By his sophomore, or second, year of high school, Johnson was 6 feet 4 inches (1.9 m) tall. He was also the starting wide receiver for his high-school team.

Calvin Johnson was not only the best player at Sandy Creek High School. Many **scouts** and football writers believed he was the top high-school player in the state of Georgia. Some even thought he was one of the 10 best in the whole nation.

In 2010, Johnson's high school retired his number to honor him. This means that no one who plays for Sandy Creek will ever again wear the number 81.

Johnson ranked first in Georgia Tech history for career receiving yards with 2,927.

Georgia Tech

Many of the top college football teams were interested in Johnson, but he decided to stay close to home. He accepted an offer from Georgia Tech to play for the Yellow Jackets. The Yellow Jackets are famous for sending future stars to the NFL. Johnson wanted to be one of those future stars.

In 2004, Johnson broke Georgia Tech's freshman records by catching 38 passes for 837 total yards and 7 **touchdowns**. He followed up with an excellent sophomore season, in which he had 54 catches, 888 yards, and 6 touchdowns. By his junior year, Johnson enjoyed a reputation as one of the top players in all of college football. Some experts and fans predicted that he might win the Heisman Trophy. This trophy is awarded each year to the college athlete with the best season. Johnson did not win the Heisman, but he did win the 2006 Fred Biletnikoff Award. This award is given each year to the best wide receiver. Johnson earned it with 76 catches, 2,012 yards, and 15 touchdowns!

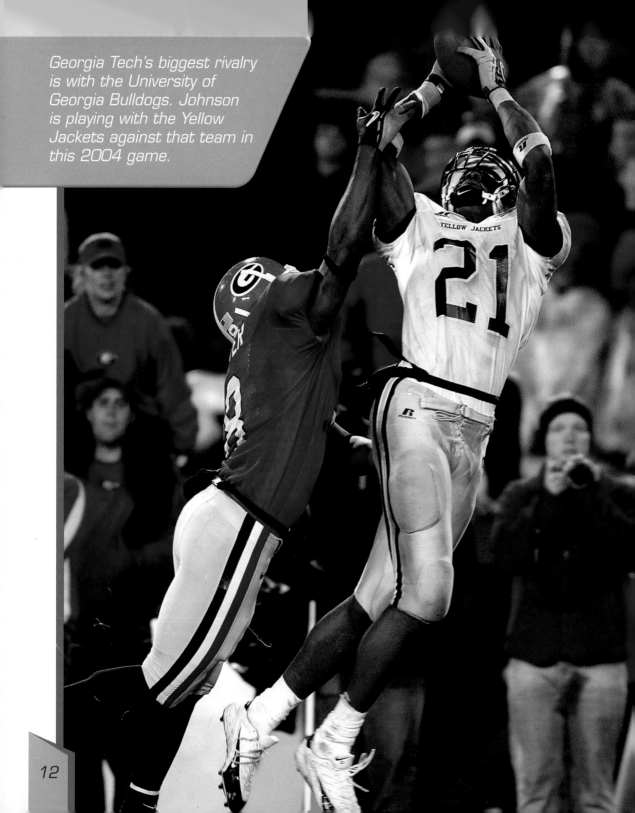

Georgia Tech's biggest rivalry is with the University of Georgia Bulldogs. Johnson is playing with the Yellow Jackets against that team in this 2004 game.

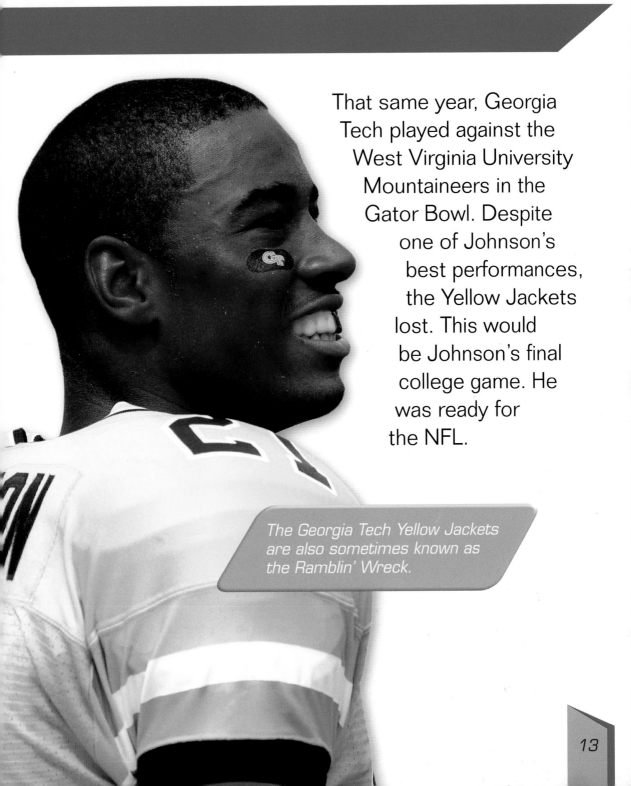

That same year, Georgia Tech played against the West Virginia University Mountaineers in the Gator Bowl. Despite one of Johnson's best performances, the Yellow Jackets lost. This would be Johnson's final college game. He was ready for the NFL.

The Georgia Tech Yellow Jackets are also sometimes known as the Ramblin' Wreck.

Drafted

The NFL holds its **draft** each spring. The NFL draft is the system through which teams pick the best new players. To make it fair, the teams with the worst records get to choose players before teams with good records. In 2007, the Detroit Lions were one of the worst teams in the NFL. They had the second overall pick in the 2007 draft, and they picked Johnson.

NFL commissioner Roger Goodell is shown here posing with Calvin Johnson after the Detroit Lions picked him in the NFL draft.

Johnson helped the Lions win this game against the Minnesota Vikings during his first season with the team.

The sports **media** reported rumors that the Lions did not mean to keep Johnson. It can take several seasons for **rookies** to become stars. The Lions had been bad for a long time. It was possible for them to trade Johnson away for stars who could improve the team now, rather than in a few seasons. Many predicted that Detroit would trade him to the Tampa Bay Buccaneers. Lions fans were delighted when they got the news that Johnson would stay in Detroit.

The Detroit sports community welcomed Johnson to his new town. A few days after the draft, Johnson appeared at a Detroit Tigers baseball game to throw out the first pitch. Fans were excited to have one of the best college football players of all time on their team. If anyone could help turn their team around, it was Johnson.

Johnson continues to lend his support to other teams in the Detroit sports community. Here, he is signing autographs at a 2012 Detroit Tigers game.

During the 2008 season, Johnson had even better stats than during his rookie season. Unfortunately, the Lions had their worst-ever season.

Zero and Sixteen

Johnson earned the nickname Megatron in his first season. His teammate and fellow wide receiver Roy Williams gave him the nickname, and it stuck with fans. Williams also gave Johnson the nickname Bolt after the Olympic Gold medalist Usain Bolt. Just like Bolt, no one could catch Johnson once he started running.

Wide receivers like Johnson are called offensive players. Offensive players try to score for their team. Defensive players try to keep the other team from scoring.

Johnson **injured** his lower back early in his rookie season. He played through the pain and had a good first year. Fans needed to be patient, though. The rest of the Detroit team was not as good as its new star receiver. The 2007 Detroit Lions finished once again with a losing record and failed to make the **play-offs**.

The Lions were even worse in 2008. They traded Roy Williams away, making Johnson the team's lead wide receiver. It takes more than one great player to make a winning team, though. As good as Johnson was, he could not win all by himself. The Lions became the first team in NFL history to finish 0 and 16. This means they lost every single game. It was a bad year for the Lions, but a good year for Johnson. He led the league in touchdowns by a receiver.

Johnson made 12 touchdowns during the 2008 season. Here he is making a touchdown in a 2008 game against the Indianapolis Colts.

Winning in Detroit

Nearly all of the Lions' coaches were fired after the team's 2008 performance. Many of the players were released. The new coaches decided to build a team around Megatron. A star wide receiver needs a star **quarterback**. Detroit set out to get one. Since the Lions were the worst team in the NFL in 2008, they had first choice in the 2009 draft. They picked star quarterback Matthew Stafford with the first pick.

With new coaches and players, the Lions improved only slightly from their winless 2008 season. They won two games. Detroit's fans were nothing if not patient. Building a winning team around Johnson and Stafford would take time. The Lions improved to 6 and 10 in the 2010 season. Once again, Johnson was the team's best player. He recorded 1,120 receiving yards and 12 touchdowns.

Here Johnson (right) is talking to teammate Tony Scheffler (left) during a 2012 game.

Johnson is watching the video replay of himself breaking Jerry Rice's record on December 22, 2012, here.

Finally, in 2011, Johnson and the Lions put together the kind of season for which fans had been waiting. Johnson recorded 1,681 receiving yards and scored 16 touchdowns. More importantly, the Lions finally had a winning season, and they reached the play-offs.

Johnson made NFL history in 2012 by breaking Jerry Rice's record of receiving yards in a single season. With 1,964 receiving yards, he fell just 36 yards short of 2,000! He also led the NFL in catches that season.

Johnson had 67 total receptions during the 2009 season. Here is a near miss during that season in a game against the Cincinnati Bengals.

Teammates Calvin Johnson (left) and Matthew Stafford (right) sometimes attend events together off the field. Here they are at the Cartoon Network Hall of Game Awards in 2012. They won the Dynamic Duo award because they play together so well.

One of the Good Guys

Calvin Johnson is a quiet leader who chooses to lead by example. Johnson knows his job is to work hard, practice football, and stay in shape. He also knows that there is more to life than football.

Johnson created his own **charity** in 2008. The Calvin Johnson Jr. Foundation helps students in poor areas of Atlanta and Detroit. The foundation awards **scholarships** to student athletes. The foundation also gives food to families in need and raises money to fight breast cancer.

Johnson is well liked both on and off the field. In fact, in 2010, his good attitude won him an honor from the local media called the Detroit Lions Good Guy Award.

All-Star Facts

During college, Johnson and a group of fellow students traveled to Bolivia. They helped build safer and cleaner latrines, or bathrooms, for people who lived in poor conditions.

Megatron Plays On

Before the 2012 season, Johnson signed a new contract with the Lions. The eight-year, $132 million deal made him the highest-paid receiver in the NFL. By the end of the season, Megatron showed that he was worth it! He was the best wide receiver in the league. He had broken Jerry Rice's record and also helped the Lions become one of the better teams in the NFL.

Before Johnson joined the Detroit Lions, other NFL teams looked forward to beating the team. Those days are over. Johnson has helped turn the Detroit Lions into a winning team.

Here Johnson makes the play in which he breaks Jerry Rice's single-season record for receiving yards.

Stat Sheet

Team: Detroit Lions
Position: Wide receiver
Number: 81
Born: September 29, 1985
Height: 6 feet 5 inches (2 m)
Weight: 236 pounds (107 kg)

Season	Team	Rushing Attempts	Rushing Yards	Rushing Touchdowns
2007	Lions	48	756	4
2008	Lions	78	1,331	12
2009	Lions	67	948	5
2010	Lions	77	1,120	12
2011	Lions	96	1,681	16
2012	Lions	122	1,964	5

Glossary

athlete (ATH-leet) Someone who takes part in sports.

charity (CHER-uh-tee) A group that gives help to the needy.

draft (DRAFT) The selection of people for a special purpose.

injured (IN-jurd) Harmed or hurt.

media (MEE-dee-uh) Journalists and people who appear on TV and radio shows.

play-offs (PLAY-ofs) Games played after the regular season ends to see who will play in the championship game.

quarterback (KWAHR-ter-bak) A football player who directs the team's plays.

rookies (RU-keez) New major-league players.

scholarships (SKAH-lur-ships) Money given to people to pay for school.

scouts (SKOWTS) People who help sports teams find new, young players.

touchdowns (TUTCH-downz) Getting the football behind the opposing team's goal line. A touchdown is worth six points.

wide receivers (WYD rih-SEE-verz) Football players whose biggest job is to catch passes from the quarterback.

Index

Websites

Due to the changing nature of Internet links, PowerKids Press has developed an online list of websites related to the subject of this book. This site is updated regularly. Please use this link to access the list: www.powerkidslinks.com/asp/cjohn/